So, You're Living for Christ in High School?

Alexis Cole

Dedication

This book is dedicated to teenagers like me that are trying to live their life for Christ while going through high school.

Contents

Introduction

The most blessed people are the ones who find Christ early on in life, especially in high school. The fact that we know that God is by our side gives us a head start in life. Sometimes it's hard to believe, but life is so much easier when you choose to follow Jesus. Now, if you are a true follower of Jesus, you know that there are many tests and trials that come your way. This book is to exemplify tests and trials of us young disciples, guide lost ones who think they're alone, and inform people who want to be one. I see high school as the best and worst time of a person's life, and this is part of my journey and what I've learned as a young disciple thus far.

Young

I remember one day when I was really young and I was feeling like I had just woken up and started living life. Crazy, I know, but I felt as if my whole childhood was just a dream and everyone else remembered it but me. I must have been only ten or eleven years old at the time, and I realized how fast life was going. "Enjoy being young while you can," older people always say. I know being young has so many benefits, but sometimes stress and the weight of the world overpowers them. The time period from birth to around fourteen years old is pretty cool, but I feel like when you're about fifteen years old (when people start high school), your perception and reception of the world changes. Our youth is a delicate time in our lives, it's the time when we build the foundation of our future.

A lot of young people come to know Christ after they've already gone through a stage in life where they are searching for who they are and for something to fulfill them. This stage typically consists of drugs, alcohol, partying, or sex. If you're like me, your stage may have not been as severe, but it was still a time in your life when you were just lost. The stage could have even happened when you were already saved, but just not spiritually mature. You may be in the stage right now, I know we all have different stories. The point is that being young has many traps. You are trying to navigate through life and figure out who you are while the devil sends so many temptations and storms.

There was a time when I almost fell into the trap. I thought to myself, "I'm young. Why don't I just focus on being young, having fun, and not caring about what I do now, and just worry about getting my life right in the future?" To a nonbeliever, I'm sure that sounded like a great idea. I knew the Lord would forgive me, but what I was not realizing was that the decisions I would make during my "free period" would dramatically alter the plans God has set aside for me. I wasn't thinking about how big of a mess I would have to clean up when I finally realized I was making one. Because of how great he is, God forgivingly realigned my focus and the devil was silenced. There's no doubt that if I were to fall into the trap it would lead me nowhere but to the grave, and I would not be the person I am today. When you do not listen to God and you do things or go places without His consent, you come in contact with challenges you were not even supposed to have. The devil is smart because he knows how we feel when we are YOUNG. The majority of us just want to feel alive, and are constantly searching for something to fill the hole inside of us. We were born into the nature that causes us to always want to go after what our flesh desires, but our flesh is opposite of our spirit. What we want is not always going to line up with what God has planned for us. When we are disciples of Christ, He fills the hole and earnestly prays that we don't fall into the trap. In the Bible, in Matthew 24, Jesus is talking to His disciples in a parable about a servant and his master. In the parable the master trusts a servant to be in charge of the other household servants and Jesus compares the result of the servant doing a good job and the servant doing a bad job. Verses

46 and 47 explain that if the servant does good, he will be put in charge of all the master owns, and verses 48 and 49 state, "But what if the servant is evil and thinks, 'My master won't be back for a while,' and begins beating the other servants, partying, and getting drunk?" As disciples, God has put us in charge of the world. We ultimately are servants that are supposed to be doing work for His Kingdom. Jesus (the master) has left, and it's up to us to do everything that he would do. It's tempting to be a bad servant and think, "Oh, Jesus probably won't be coming back for a long time. I'll just live life the way I see fit for now, and then try to get right with God when I'm older." We must be careful if this thought comes to our minds because it can lead us down a road that takes forever to see a way to make a U-turn. I also remember thinking one time about all of the adults I had heard testimonies from and how almost all of them included wild teenage years, and I thought, "Why do I have to have my life together right now? Jesus delivered them, so I know he'll deliver me." One of the things I love about God is how patient he is because no matter how many times I question him, he constantly and lovingly gets me back on track and tells me straight up, "Alexis, your story is not going to line up with everyone else's. You are fortunate to have your life together in a way that you are focused on the right things. Do you really think they were happy without me? Yes, it was fun for them to live wildly for a minute and feel 'alive,' but at the end of the day the void continues and they were alone. Don't think for a second that just because you're young there will be enough time for you to prove to me that you love me and

4

that I won't use you to lead people to the kingdom of God. I know you feel like you got such a long way ahead of you, but the longer and harder the journey is, the more treasure that awaits."

Being young comes with so many distractions. In high school there's grades, friendships, relationships, and sports to worry about. Distractions make it so easy to stray from God and to forget to read the Bible, pray, and worship on a daily basis. Heather Lindsey, founder of the Pinky Promise Movement, preached to me one day in one of her YouTube videos and said that our youth is not to be distracted by the cares of this world, our youth is for developing our spiritual maturity. We do this by earnestly seeking God, praying, reading, and working for God's kingdom. There was a season in my life when I would totally forget about God for the seven hours that I was at school. I only prayed at night, I didn't really read my Bible unless I was at church, and I didn't necessarily do work for the kingdom of God. I was wasting my time as a follower because I wasn't actually following and seeking God. I was worried about what all the creations were doing and what they thought about me rather than praising the creator. God wants you to know that spiritual maturity doesn't have to wait until you're older, he wants your heart now.

I used to think that because I was young I couldn't be used for God's kingdom and wouldn't be taken seriously if I tried. Thoughts like, "That person isn't going to listen to me when I try to help them fix their life, I'm only a teenager," or "They will think I'm a joke if I try to pray for them," or "They don't want/need my help," would come to my mind. God helped me realize that I could not listen to the lie the devil tried to whisper in my ear because the word of God told me otherwise. In the Bible, 2 Kings 22:1 states, "Josiah was eight years old when he became king, and he reigned in Jerusalem thirty-one years" God used someone as young as eight years old to help fix a broken city. King Amon, the king before Josiah, was evil and did evil things in the eyes of the Lord as 2 Kings 21:20 tell us and 2 Kings 22:2 tells us that King Josiah did what was right in the eyes of the Lord. If God can use what would be a third grader in our day to turn around a whole city, just imagine what he could do with a kid who knows a little more about life, that is surrounded by the most lost people in the world from 8 am to 3 pm every day, and who's heart is full of the love of Christ. God used Josiah for a city, what if He wants to use you for your school? When I imagine young disciples trying to do work for God's kingdom, I think of the story of David and Goliath in 1 Samuel 17 of the Bible. The Philistines and the Israelites were in a war, and Goliath, who was part of the Philistines' army, shouted to the Israelites telling them to pick one of their soldiers to fight him. Now, the Bible tells us that Goliath was over nine feet tall and wore armor that weighed about as much as a teenage girl, therefore, no Israelite soldier was exactly jumping in line to fight him. David, who was a shepherd and the youngest of his brothers, was sent by his father to the camp to give food to his brothers. Once David picked up on the situation, he proclaimed that he would fight Goliath. Everyone of course laughed and doubted him, but David stood firm because he knew the Lord was with him. The Bible tells us that David told Goliath, "You come to me with sword, spear, and javelin, but I come to you in the name of the Lord of Heaven's Armies - the God of the Armies of Israel, whom you have defied" (1 Samuel 17:45). David then went on to defeat Goliath with a stone and a sling. When we worry about what people will think of us, whether or not we will succeed, and how many Goliath's there will be when we try to do something for God's kingdom, we miss the opportunity to show people who God is. David was just like us, a young disciple who's heart was full of the love of Christ, but a trait that he had that some of us forget to have is the absence of fear because of faith in God. It didn't matter that David was young, all that mattered was that he knew God was with him and was willing to face something as big as Goliath for the army of God.

Everyone starts to face the world as soon as they are born. Certainly everyone has different tests and trials, and young disciples undergo similar ones, especially in high school. It can be hard sometimes if you're the only Christ follower in the group or if you feel like all the good you're trying to do isn't getting you anywhere. Sometimes it may seem like a lot of people are getting blessed, but you're the one that's living right. There may be times that come that just make you ready to be with Jesus. When we're young, we're expected to have the most stamina, be the happiest, make mistakes and learn from them, be without stress, make our parents proud, and set an example for those even younger than us. Life can get a little overwhelming for young people, too. Just because we don't have bills to pay, mouths to feed, and a shelter to provide, doesn't mean that we don't feel the weight of the world as well. I'm not saying that adults do not have much more things to worry about than teenagers do, but it can still be challenging for teens to endure the brokenness of the world. Even though some adults may not find this justifiable, it is no surprise that the Bible justifies it in the book of Isaiah. Isaiah is comforting the people of Israel (God's people) when he says, "Even youths grow tired and weary, and young men stumble and fall; but those who hope in the Lord will renew their strength. They will soar on wings like eagles; they will run and not grow weary, they will walk and not be faint" (Isaiah 40:30-31). God knows that it can be hard sometimes. He understands that we feel pressure because we want to do what's right in His eyes. But, as the scripture states, we must come to GOD (not our friends, not our parents, not social media, not Netflix, not food, not anything of this worlds) to renew our strength so we can keep fighting the good fight. We are the CHOSEN generation!

Easy

I am not proud of it, but one day I found myself thinking, "Would it just be easier if I didn't follow Christ and just lived life the way I wanted?" It was a thought the devil placed in my head. Just like Adam and Eve, he wanted me to feel like I didn't need God, that I could be like him in a way in which I didn't have to rely on anyone and could carry this world on my shoulders by myself. Thankfully, I snapped out of my unfaithful moment with a quickness and reminded myself that dwelling in this world full of brokenness alone would not be easier for it would be deathly. It's a reason why people commit suicide. Whether or not they fail or succeed, suicidal people experience the weight of the world, just like everyone else that has a "normal" life, but the difference is that they do not know there is a God who longs to hear from them, who longs to save them if they would just reach out and seek him. They never come in contact with the true love of God, and it's not always their fault. In John 16 of the Bible, Jesus is warning His disciples about leaving them to be persecuted. Jesus comforts them by informing them that they will not be alone, for He will send an advocate (what Christians know as the Holy Spirt) to be with them and guide them. What really sticks out to me is that in verse 33 Jesus says, "I have told you these things, so that in me you may have peace. In this world you will have trouble. But take heart! I have overcome the world." Jesus tells us upfront that just because we follow him and live according to

God's will, doesn't mean that our life will be easy. But what makes clear is that we do not have to endure it alone. "I have overcome the world," He says. What does that mean? To me that means that anything in this world that comes for me or tries to attack or alter my life and spirit, Jesus has already overcome. So why should I fear? If you're in high school, you probably experience multiple daily challenges. The devil knows that you want to spread the love of Christ to people, so out of spite, he provokes that person to look at you a certain way, or that teacher to give you a bad grade, or that person you've been trying so hard to forgive to do something else that makes you want to lose sight of who you are representing. There have been multiple times when I would ask the Lord, "Why can't I feel your spirit all the time? I don't want to be angry. I don't want to be upset. I don't want to feel some type of way towards that person," but then I realized that if that was the case, life would just be easy and my spirit wouldn't grow.

You see the word "easy" does not line up with the word of God. If life was easy, why would we need God? That doesn't mean that there won't be times in our lives where everything is going good and we thrive. But what I've noticed is that there always comes a storm, whether mild or severe, that forces us not only to lean on God, but to grow. Living for Christ in high school is like a new army recruit trying to get through the first week of boot camp. It's just like I want to fast forward through all of the hard stuff and be at the point where I'm happily married with kids and a career, just like an army recruit wants to fast forward from civilian to soldier. I always have to remind myself

10

that I have to keep moving in this journey in order for God to grow and prepare me to become the Godly woman who is ready to fulfill her purpose, become a serving wife, and a nurturing mother. In the same way a recruit has to go through boot camp to be prepared for war. In this life, our spirits are always going to have to fight; therefore, it is necessary to let God prepare us NOW, before giving us responsibilities that we will try to sustain without proper training. It may not feel great right now but the promising end feels so much greater than the challenging beginning. In the Bible, Paul wrote, "I consider that our present sufferings are not worth comparing with the glory that will be revealed to us" (Romans 8:18). I believe the main picture Paul was trying to paint was that whatever we go through in this life will not compare to the glory that will be revealed in heaven, but I also believe that it can be applied to when we are still living in this world. I take it as all of the hard work I have put in to get good grades, all of the times I have to go clock in to an hourly job, and all of the nights spent alone will absolutely not compare to the all of the work I get to put in to feed into other people's lives, all the mornings I will wake up and do what I love to do, and all of the nights spent with the family that I prayed and served for.

One of the best servants of the Lord in the Bible is known as John the Baptist. John the Baptist did something every day that was not easy, and that was tell everyone he could about Jesus. The book of Matthew tells us that plenty of people went to John and were baptized by him in the Jordan River. He was even so fortunate to baptize Jesus!

In Matthew 3:11, John is talking to the Pharisees and Sadducees when he says, "I baptize you with water for repentance. But after me comes one who is more powerful than I, whose sandals I am not worthy to carry. He will baptize you with the Holy Spirit and fire." Part of living for Christ is telling people about Him. John the Baptist made it look easy in a way. He told people what was up without worrying about what they would say, how they would feel, or what would happen to him. Jesus wants all of us disciples to tell people about Him and preach the gospel like John did, but it seems to be so hard to me and I know I am not alone. When in high school, the thought of what people are going to think about you is constantly running through your head. Teenagers can not only be so judgmental but just plain cruel. It can be so hard to try to witness to a fellow classmate about Jesus because you never know how they are going to react, what they are going to say, who they are going to tell, what they are going to think, and if it will even be planted on good ground. For the most part, I do not care about what other people think of me, because it's really none of my business and I know God loves me no matter who I am or what I do. But there is still a part of me that makes me scared when it comes to telling people about Christ. It's easy to think about, but anytime I've been in the moment I've thought, "They're gonna think I'm crazy." This does not give me an excuse in any way, I am just trying to be transparent with you so that you can see that I am as imperfect as you. No matter how hard it was (and is), John the Baptist did what he was called to do, what we are all called to do. Because of John's such brave discipleship, Jesus honored him and told a crowd in Matthew 11:11, "Truly I tell you, among those born of woman there has not risen anyone greater than John the Baptist; yet whoever is least in the kingdom of heaven is greater than he." Jesus called John the greatest man born of a woman all because John simply told people about Him. Let me remind you that some of Jesus' disciples healed people just like Him, but it only takes the simple task of telling people about the glory of God for us to be seen as great. "It's not that easy," I still say to myself, but the good thing about hard stuff is that once you do it a couple times, it becomes a little less hard.

I remember talking to my mother one day saying, "life is hard." It was probably one of those times when I'm feeling discouraged about something, randomly feeling depressed, or my heart's hearting for somebody. I cannot remember what my mother said, it was probably something like, "yeah," or she might have tried to encourage me, but failingly said, "no it's not." The point is that she didn't really know what I needed in that moment. She did not understand how I felt, just like some people do not understand why us disciples feel in love with someone we've never seen. When you really invite Jesus into your life, your whole world changes, your heart is softened, and your mind is renewed. You see things in a way that unbelievers cannot. This can be hard because it makes it hard for people to understand you. They don't get why you just won't say a small curse word. They don't see why it's important to treat everyone the best way possible. They don't understand why you're not having sex until you get married, why you won't send nudes, and why you won't try to get into a relationship with that unequally yoked boy or girl. Part of what makes representing Christ challenging is the other people that are not. Because they do not have a relationship with Christ, they will not know how to love you, how to treat you, how to speak to you, and how you feel. It makes not only high school but life hard because you want them to get it so badly, and it would just be so much easier if they just understood that a time comes when we will have to give an account for what we did with the life we were given. I used to say, "Lord, why can't they just understand that I love you, and because I love you I don't want to gossip about that person, or go to that party, or lie to my parents?" or whatever battle I was fighting with my flesh at the time because people just couldn't seem to get it. We can't complain though because like I mentioned earlier Jesus tells us upfront that we will have trouble in this world and we can't fret because He tells us that He has overcome this world. Believe it or not, Jesus' disciples went through things back then while trying to follow Him that are similar to the things we go through now. In Matthew 24, Jesus is again being transparent with His disciples and telling them about everything they will go through because they choose to follow Him. What comforts and strengthens me is after Jesus finishes the list of battles we will face, He says in verse 13, "but the one who stands firm to the end will be saved." Living for Christ isn't the hard part, it's representing Him when hurt in life comes our way. High school may not be easy, but a diploma is worth learning for. This life may not be easy, but the kingdom of God is worth fighting for. Stand firm, young disciples, who knows where we would be if Jesus didn't.

Purpose

Everybody is asked the question, "What do you want to be when you grow up?" at least once in their life. In high school, guidance counselors constantly provide career search help. As Christians, we understand that God has set aside a specific "job" for us that correlates to why we are on this Earth. We understand that He has a purpose for all of us. Although God has a specific reason for each of us being here, we all share one common purpose. In the Bible, Jesus is talking to His disciples when He proclaims, "Therefore, go and make disciples of all the nations, baptizing them in the name of the Father and the Son and the Holy Spirit" (Matthew 28:19). As Christians, our main purpose is to do our very best to lead people to Christ. As I stated earlier, in high school this can be difficult because of all of the insecurities the devil tries to put in our heads, we must always try to push aside our feelings because there are people out there that are waiting for us to fulfill our purpose. God knows that it may be hard to approach the quiet girl in class who dresses in all black or the boy who always disrupts class and talks down to other people, but He also knows that those people are hurting and He has called US to lead them to Him. If my parents send me to the store to get some milk, that's exactly what I'm going to bring back to them. If God sent us to this Earth to bring him lost and broken people, that's exactly what we need to do. I'm not saying that there aren't times when you mess up, say the wrong thing, or don't say anything at all, because not a single human is perfect and I, for one, do not jump at every opportunity to lead somebody to Christ. Scripture says that we all have fallen short of the glory of God, but we must realize that God's purpose for us is so much bigger than us. If we do not fulfill it, it will affect more than just OUR life and relationship with God.

After high school, the world expects us to go to college, get a degree, and ultimately get a job to provide for ourselves. That is an ideal path that some of us may be called to go down, but whatever profession God calls you in, He will use you in. God may call you to be a preacher, doctor, police officer, teacher, musician, singer, or even a stay-at-home parent. A great way of figuring it out is examining your gifts, but keep in mind that your gifts do not provide a barrier around the width in which God will use you.

I believe that God has this big, main purpose for all of us, and along the way, He calls us to do different tasks that will lead us to where we need to be. Whatever God calls you to do, He will equip you to do. I personally do not like English. In school, I hate doing essays, discussion forums, lab reports, and basically anything that forces me to write because I'm not the best at grammar and punctuation. The gift that God gave me is math, but yet right now, He is equipping me to write this book because He has called me to encourage teenagers in this world like me. That doesn't mean I'm going to be writing books all my life, but writing this book was a job God gave me in which I had to trust Him. Your purpose is going to require faith in God. All of it is not just going to suddenly appear. You have to have faith that the work God started within you will be finished. There are certain things you may have to go through in order to fully carry out the plan He has for your life. We cannot be afraid because God expects us to understand that He will help us breathe in the waves that He tells us to swim through. He may call one of His young disciples to do something that may be seen as peculiar in the eyes of a non-follower, but we have to be willing to trust Him when nobody believes in us and thinks we're crazy.

Like a typical teenager, I started working at my first job while in high school. I got my first job the summer after my freshman year at Chick-fil-A. Although Chick-fil-A is a great company for various reasons, working there wasn't exactly the highlight of my life. When you start working in the world and dealing with different types of people, it changes your perception. There were multiple days when I said, "I do not like people," at least one time in my shift. It wasn't always the customers that would alter my spirit, but fellow employees could be a pain as well. It got to a point to where I really dreaded going to work, therefore, after I earned enough money to buy my car, I quit. I got a new job at Five Guys Burgers and Fries thinking that it would be better. Although it wasn't nearly as busy as Chick-fil-A was, I still faced some of the same battles. I worked at Five Guys for about three months until I made the decision to quit and start working at Olive Garden. I made the decision to work at Olive Garden based on the fact that I was going to get paid more, one of my friends was also going to start working there, and I felt like it was going to be easier. After a few weeks of working at Olive Garden, I realized that I was going to be challenged everywhere I went. God opened my eyes to see how much I had tried to make my own path in life rather than follow His. I went from job to job each time thinking that the next one would be better, rather than being faithful with the first job that I prayed for. I made decisions based off of my feelings, rather than God's plan. Each time I kept wanting more and more. I wanted more money, more benefits, nicer bosses, fewer difficult customers, and more of what would just satisfy me. The more I worked these part-time jobs, the more I wanted to just fast forward to having a career and fulfilling the purpose God has for me. God shifted my focus one day when I saw a verse in the Bible that Jesus had said when He was telling His disciples a parable about three servants, saying, "To those who use well what they are given, even more will be given, and they will have an abundance. But from those who do nothing, even what little they have will be taken away" (Matthew 25:29). I was tested more at Olive Garden than I ever was at my first two jobs. God showed me that I had to be faithful with little and what He initially blesses me with in order for Him to bless me with more. How could He trust me with a career if I couldn't be faithful with a part-time job? Often times in high school, we see our goals and we want to snap our fingers and get there. But God uses things such as rude customers, cranky employees, spiteful teammates, or whatever else that you have to face that is stalling your purpose to prepare you for your purpose. One of my bosses at Olive Garden often made me get out of my spirit so much that I wanted to quit yet another job. Later on, I was shown in the Bible that Ecclesiastes 10:4 says, "If your boss is angry at you, don't quit! A quiet spirit can overcome even great mistakes." Whatever your "angry boss" is that makes you want to quit and not be faithful to where God has placed you, whether it's a job, internship, sports team, or club, I encourage you to stay and pray because believe me, God wants us to begin fulfilling our purpose way more than we do, heaven is relying on it.

As I stated earlier, I do pretty well at math in school. God has shown me that my purpose in life is to be a high school math teacher. I believe that He's going to use me to reach teens before they go out into world living on their own. Whether or not the Lord has revealed to you your purpose, in Jesus' name, DO NOT let the devil or someone on this earth try to distort your view of it or stop you from fulfilling it. Not everyone is going to understand and appreciate what God has planned for you to do, but you must stand firm when you are completely sure you know what it is. It might take time and you might have to try different things until you figure it out but letting someone else try to decide it for you is one of the biggest mistakes you can make. Because I do so well in school, people are often baffled when I tell them I want to be a high school teacher. They try to change my mind saying, "Oh, you'll be broke" or "You can do so much more with your brains," without even realizing how they can affect me with what they are saying. It never really shook my foundation until the second semester of my junior year. In the very beginning of 2018, I, Alexis Cole, was questioning my purpose because I let other people alter my view.

Teaching all of sudden seemed small to me. I was falling into a trap and was about to mess up not only my life, but the lives I'm supposed to change. I literally made up this whole new purpose in my mind that did not come from God at all. I made myself believe that I was called to be a model. I wanted to be some type of sports model for a brand like Nike or Adidas. It did not make sense whatsoever because first of all, I have never been that confident, especially not enough to be a model, second of all, I do not like attention, third of all, I am too smart to not go to college, and finally, I had doubt. At the time it made sense in my head because I felt like God was going to work through my insecurities and put me on a platform to be role model to other girls like me. Thankfully, God used my dad to speak to me and when I was telling my dad about my "new purpose," I realized that I was hesitant. It was almost like I wasn't proud of it. I'm not saying that there is anything wrong with being a model, of course, but I knew deep down that it was not what the Lord had called me to do, and it took saying it aloud to realize it. My dad reassured that feeling because he reminded me of all the characteristics of my personality and how they were all characteristics a teacher needed, not a model, and that being a model would only be serving me, not the Lord. He also told me that the fact that I had doubt almost definitely meant that it was not my purpose. God showed me that He prepares us for the part we are supposed to play. I started acting like I was a teacher and playing school with my cousins at a very young age, just like my brother (who is now a famous Christian rapper/singer) who started rapping when he was really young (four years old to be exact). The work He puts within us way before we are born grows until He knows we are ready for it to blossom. The people that may try to tell you things different from what God has already confirmed can be your teachers, counselors, and even your own family and friends, but you must stand firm on your foundation. They don't know that what they say has the power to affect the kingdom of God if you listen. Looking back, I realize that part of what made me question my purpose was jealousy of other's. I would look on the internet and social media and see all these powerful Christian leaders fulfilling their purpose in front of big crowds and it made me feel like my purpose wasn't as good as theirs. God quickly helped me realize that we are all the same. He has called us to do different things, but none of our purposes are seen as less than in the kingdom of God. Yes, some people are famous performers or big-time preachers, but a high school teacher can change just as many lives as they can. God doesn't assign any "wack" jobs, because, ultimately, they are all working towards the same thing. If you grow up and have a moment like my modeling situation and are confused because God's not funding some business you decided to start, providing gigs for your new acting career, or making a way out of no way for a purpose you made up in your head, take a step back and asses your heart and motives because God will not fund or provide for something He did not call you to do. If, during that step back, God assures you that what you are striding towards is your true purpose, keep striving, but if not, keep praying. Often times, we can get caught up thinking about all that we are capable of doing rather than what God really wants us to do. Pastor Michael Todd, head pastor of Transformation Church, explained it as: We start striding to reach our potential rather than our purpose. God is a great God that blesses each of us with multiple gifts, but don't feel like you have show them all and be "the best of the best" to earn favor in the Lord's eyes.

Just because God calls us to do something doesn't mean that it will come easily. My dad and brother (Aaron Cole) worked for over fourteen years to get my brother to where he is now. Of course he wouldn't have gotten anywhere without Christ, but it took an inner hustle for him to not only to achieve his dream, but to also fulfill his purpose. There are times when I don't feel like working hard. Like I've been saying, I'm always wanting things to fast forward, but what always renews my strength is 2 Corinthians 4:16-18. Paul is writing to the church of God in Corinth when he says, "Therefore we do not lose heart. Though outwardly we are wasting away, yet inwardly we are being renewed day by day. For our light and momentary troubles are achieving for us an eternal glory that far outweighs them all. So, we fix our eyes not on what is seen, but on what is unseen, since what is seen is temporary, but what is unseen is eternal." I know when I get to college, there's probably going to be a class that kicks my butt. When you start striding towards your purpose, the devil is going to attack you in some way. I encourage you to not focus on how hard life may be sometimes, the times when you're confused because all you are trying to do is live for Christ and do His will. Walking towards purpose is going to involve some bumps in the road that cause you to trip, but like

Paul says we have to keep our eyes fixed on what is unseen. I've experienced the bumps just while writing this book, believe me the devil hates when we do work for Christ's kingdom, but, young disciples, keep hustling, because the temporary battles you have to face at school, at home, at work, or wherever they may come will not compare to the glory that will be revealed. Our purpose is treasure.

Identity

High school is a time when we start to find out who we really are. As students, we are tested daily in so many ways. Whether we are kind, rude, smart, not so smart, loving, hateful, proactive, lazy, and so many other characteristics that make up our identity. As disciples of Christ, who we are is supposed to represent who Christ is. It took me until I got to high school to realize that my identity was in Him. I realized I would not be the beautiful person I am if it wasn't for Him. I am not calling myself beautiful to be conceited, I know who I am and that I am beautiful because God made me and I live for Him. When you're living for Christ and your heart is changed and you're just feeling His spirit and feel love for people, it shows. People will notice the beauty within you and sometimes will even tell you. I remember two friends of mine tell me at two different times, "Alexis, you're a beautiful person." Although it did pump my head up just a little bit (Lord, forgive me), them saying that to me opened my eyes to see that what was in me had the power to actually touch people. It helped me realize that I was beautiful because of Christ because when they said that to me the only explanation that came to my mind was the love of Christ within me. Paul writes in 2 Corinthians 4:7 saying, "We now have this light shining in our hearts, but we ourselves are like fragile clay jars containing this great treasure. This makes it clear that our great power is from God, not from ourselves." This scripture speaks loudly, telling me that my body is just some fragile jar that would break if it were dropped, but with Christ, behind my veil of brokenness is treasure. The power inside us to touch people is not from us, but from God. As young disciples, our identity and the power within us is treasure, and so many people are searching for it whether they know it or not. They just don't know that the word of God is the map.

Another way one could explain the term "identity," is the way one is described. Although we are mostly described by our physical appearance, our internal attributes are what someone would really need to know to figure out who we are. People will usually describe us by what they see and what they see usually represents who we are. Notice that I said, "usually" because I'm not talking about that person that has made up their own perception of you based on their judgmental or jealous feelings. Of course not everyone is going to like you, that's just life. I'm talking about the people closest to you. What do you think they would have to say about you? How would they describe your personality? Would they say you're a positive person, someone loyal, a giver, a do-gooder, and, most importantly, someone who loves? Jesus says in John 13:35 when speaking to His disciples, "Your love for one another will prove to the world that you are my disciples." Love is a key characteristic of our identity because Jesus tells us that without love, no one would know that we belong to Him. Every day we are growing and developing and you have to ask yourself: Do I love the person who always has an attitude with me? Do I love the teacher who doesn't try to help me? Do I show enough love that lets people know that I belong to Christ? Am I really who I say I am? It's so hard in high school because test after test comes. We deal with people who are more grown up than they were in middle school, but still feed off of drama and hurt people to cover up their own hurt and insecurities. Teenagers can be so stubborn and my flesh doesn't want to be the type of person who loves the unlovable, but the Holy Spirit tells me that that's who I'm supposed to be. That's exactly what Christ did when He was on this Earth and He's the lamp we are supposed to shine for. When people look at you from afar, do they see the light of your spirit or the dullness of your flesh? Do they see fruit being produced from you walk with God or are you spiritually barren?

I was watching a sermon on Youtube one day, and one thing I learned from Pastor Mike Todd is that all followers of Christ share a characteristic that makes up our identity. We are all righteous. We are not righteous because we do "right" things, but we have been made righteous through Christ, therefore, we do right things.

Our identity is essentially what's inside of us. It's what's deep down in our hearts. Sometimes, we get caught up in wanting to look right. We want other people to see us in a way that is different from who we truly are. Sometimes we are guilty of putting on this makeup that presents who we try to be, but we have to realize that what people see on the outside does not matter if it does not match up on the inside. You can be physically beautiful, but if you're not beautiful on the inside, you're ugly and God don't like ugly. We can feed ourselves all these lies about who we are, but if it doesn't line up with our heart, what good is it? In the Bible, Jesus says in Mark 7:15, "It's not what goes into your body that defiles you; you are defiled by what comes from your heart." The Bible talks a lot about our heart, and I think it is important in determining who we are because without it we cannot live. Our heart is what stores all of the love we are supposed to share. Everything we say, do, and think comes from our heart. I wish I had a heart as pure as Jesus's because the way He loved was powerful enough to keep all of us from going to hell. The world likes to identify us by our physical appearance, but God identifies us by our heart. If you're struggling to figure out who you are, assess your heart. Think, what kind of heart do I have? Jesus tells us in Luke 6:45, "A good person produces good things from the treasury of a good heart, and an evil person produces evil things from the treasury of an evil heart. What you say flows from what is in your heart." People will know who you are usually by the way you speak and by the way you act. The scripture says "produces" because everything we do has an outcome. If we have a good heart, then out comes love, blessings, and encouragement. But, if we have an evil heart, then out comes hate, hurt, and brokenness. One would know something is a well if it pours out water, just as one would know you have a good heart if you pour out good things.

Earlier I said that people can usually figure out who you are by what you say, and I said "usually" because sometimes words can be empty. In the Bible, the Pharisees were guilty of this and Jesus convicted them saying, "You hypocrites! Isaiah was right when he prophesied about you: 'These people honor me with their lips, but their hearts are far from me'" (Matthew 15:7-8). As young disciples, we cannot fall into the trap of being hypocritical and saying things that we do not practice. I cannot tell you to love if I don't love. Again, it all traces back to our heart. I also said earlier that people can figure out who we are as people by what we do. Jesus justifies this when He says, "Yes, just as you can identify a tree by its fruit, so you can identify people by their actions" (Matthew 7:20). How do you act when someone has something smart to say to you or calls you out of your name? If our identity is in Christ, we should do as He would have done, but Lord knows it's not always that easy. It's so easy for me to pop off when someone treats me in a way that I don't think I should be treated and I have to remind myself that Jesus was treated the worst when all He did was walk around teaching and healing people. In the Bible, John the Baptist tells us, "Prove by the way you live that you have repented of your sins and turned to God" (Matthew 3:8). If we identify as children of God, we should prove it. We should act right, speak life, and love. If you're sitting there thinking that you're too deep into your false identity to come to life with your real one, be like David in the Bible asking God for forgiveness saying, "Create in me a clean heart, O God. Renew a loyal spirit within me" (Psalms 51:10). If you're sitting there thankful that you know that your identity is in Christ, be like David and say, "I praise you because I am fearfully and wonderfully made; your works are wonderful, I know that full well" (Psalms 139:14). Identity is not just about what type of person you are, it's also about who you're representing and why. High school can make it so easy to forget but we have to remember that we represent Christ because He loves us and died on the cross for us. I encourage you to stay true to who you are and who Christ wants you to be. Use your clean heart and produce good things.

Body of Christ

Every follower of Jesus in the world is a part of the "Body of Christ." In the Bible, Paul starts to explain it as he is writing to the church of Corinth saying, "Just as a body, though one, has many parts, but all its many parts form one body, so it is with Christ" (1 Corinthians 12:12). All of the disciples in the world each have a part to play in the body of Christ, and when one part suffers or is falling short, the whole body suffers. Sometimes it can hurt when you have a Christian friend that does something or starts doing things that doesn't line up with the word of God. I used to think I was just dramatic when my heart would hurt when one of my Christian friends would curse or begin to be impure until I read and understood this chapter. Don't get me wrong, I don't judge my fellow disciples for, of course, I know that no one is perfect and their sin is no different than my sin, but it just hurts because the kingdom of God suffers. Why would an unbeliever change if they see a believer acting in the same behavior? Paul makes it clear when he says, "Now you are the body of Christ, and each one of you is a part of it" (1 Corinthians 12:27). To be metaphorical, if your brain is infected with cancer, your whole body is going to suffer. It's kinda the same thing as an AA group of alcoholics. If one of the recovering alcoholics relapses, it makes it harder for the other ones to believe they can stay sober. The body of Christ signifies that us disciples are all in this together. When one of us does something that would upset God, it sometimes upsets us as well. One time, I found out that one of my Jesus-following friends had done something that no longer made her fully pure, and although she felt extremely bad and ashamed about it, I found myself feeling betrayed. It's not like I wanted to judge her because I know we all make mistakes, but it just hurt me because I knew God was hurting, we were supposed to be in it together, and I started to feel like I was alone. I felt like an army recruit whose buddies weren't making it through boot camp. Of course I wasn't actually alone and we all make mistakes that make us fall short of the glory of God, but the point is that when we do, it hurts the body of Christ. Because of all of the temptations in high school, it's hard to always represent Christ to the best of our abilities. This does not give us an excuse, but it is important to be real to become real. What I mean by that is that it is important for us to be aware and address our shortcomings in order for us to become a true body of Christ. I absolutely do not always do things the way Christ would, but I'm going to keep trying because I know the body of Christ depends on it. We. Are. One.

Although we are all a part of one body, we are all different. I used to think that something was wrong with me if God didn't talk to me in the same way He talked to another follower or if I wasn't used in the way someone else was used. In the Bible, Paul writes,

> Now if the foot should say, 'Because I am not a hand, I do
> not belong to the body,' it would not for that reason stop
> being part of the body. And if the ear should say, 'Because
> I am not an eye, I do not belong to the body,' it would not

for that reason stop being part of the body. If the whole body were an eye, where would the sense of hearing be? If the whole body were an ear, where would the sense of smell be? But, in fact, God has placed the parts in the body, every one of them, just as he wanted them to be (1 Corinthians 12:15-18).

God had to show me that even though all of us disciples share one purpose, our walk with Him will be different from each other's. Every part of the body functions differently, but together it's still a body. I had to realize that if God was using me at the time, it didn't mean that I was worth less. If you're sitting a table working with your hands, eventually you'll need to get up and use your legs.

Set Apart

Because we are disciples of Christ, we are significantly different from all the other people in the world. We walk differently, we talk differently, we think differently, we act differently, we see things differently, and we love differently. We are set apart from unbelievers. In the Bible, Jesus is teaching to crowds with His disciples, and He tells His followers, "You are the light of the world-like a city on a hilltop that cannot be hidden" (Matthew 5:14). After I first read this scripture, I started to fear that people saw me like everyone else. I wasn't sure if I was actually being a light in my high school. I knew my heart was different, but were my actions? Of course I wasn't going around pushing kids, disrespecting teachers, and being a bully, but did I stop the ones who were? The definition of "light" is the natural agent that simulates sight and makes things visible. We are supposed to make the love of Christ **visible**. This light we have within us, we can't hide it. What good would it be to light up a lamp then put it under the table? I know it can be very hard because usually I just want to be chill. I don't want to draw attention to myself and be seen as the "goody to shoes" that nobody wants to be around. It's selfish because it causes me to put myself and my own insecurities before the children of God. I also often let my surroundings alter my spirit. Sometimes, I adapt to whatever atmosphere I'm in instead of bringing the presence of God into every atmosphere. It's a struggle and God is still working on me because other teens will not be drawn to Christ if they do not see the ones already following Him making a difference.

One thing that has helped my walk with Christ is my youth group called, "Rooted Youth Church." One day, my youth pastor preached a message that helped me examine if I was really set apart. Pastor Lindsey Melton asked our group, "Do you change the temperature when you walk in the room?" As disciples of Christ we have an anointing and it has the power to turn bad vibes into good vibes. Just like the saying "bad company corrupts good character," our good character should corrupt devilish spirits within people in a way that encourages them to be set apart just like us. In the Bible, Jesus teaches, "All the nation will be gathered in his presence, and he will separate the people as a shepherd separates the sheep from goats" (Matthew 25:32). I might want to be the G.O.A.T. (Greatest of All Time) at a lot of things, but when it comes to the kingdom of God I need to be a sheep. Jesus explains that the sheep will be placed at His right hand and the goats on His left. The ones on the right represent the disciples that followed Christ and did things according to His word, and the ones on the left represent the people that lived according to their own will. If I'm being honest, sometimes it's difficult to be a sheep, because we don't always want to do what God tells us to do. I certainly would not be excited if God told me to help a girl who always has an attitude, with her homework, or give her a ride to school if I saw her walking. My flesh wants to do what a goat would probably do, but my spirit must be set apart to help the helpless, love the unlovable, and forgive the unforgivable.

In high school it is cliché knowledge that if you fit in, you're cool, but if you're different, you can forget it. Some people just do not like it if you are your own person. They didn't like it either back when Jesus was alive, the only difference now is they can't crucify us for it! It can be hard being who you are when everyone else around you is different. There aren't exactly a lot of people at my school that would exchange a party for Bible study on a Friday night, or any night for that matter. This generation's version of high school can be the worst time of someone's life because we are always being defined by how we look, what clothes we wear, how many likes we get on our Instagram post, and other irrelevant factors. At one point, I found myself just not wanting to go. It wasn't the actual schoolwork that was causing me stress, it was the people. But one Wednesday night in Rooted Youth Church, God made it clear to me that I don't go to school for me. I go to school because there is something inside me that everyone needs. Your kind, Christ-filled spirit could be what keeps someone on this earth another day. Not everyone is going to appreciate it, of course, the Bible tells us in Matthew 10:22, "And all nations will hate you because you are my followers. But everyone who endures to the end will be saved." People typically do not appreciate it when they feel like you are better than them, whether you feel the same way or not. There are types of people that would despise you for your pureness. They will notice you are different, think you are superior, automatically assume that you think you are superior as well, and then decide that they do not like you.

face palm All we can do is pray for those types of people. I've also had peers that would try to provoke me to do things that go against the word of God just because they know it opposes what I'm working for. I remember a friend pressuring me to cuss saying, "Just say every word in the book, just once." It's like I said before, our pureness convicts them and they don't like it, therefore, they try to make us like them. It can get tiresome because sometimes I do want to cuss somebody out or fight somebody. But my fear of the Lord is greater than my worldly desires. Sometimes, being set apart will cause you to feel alone. It's like you're trying to stay sober and everyone else is constantly drinking. I often feel like no one understands me or understands the severity of my lifestyle. I've already confessed that there was a time when I wished that I could be like everyone else and now I know that doesn't make me special. Being set apart and a child of God is a privilege because we all fail Him daily especially under the pressures high school puts on us and He doesn't have to forgive us but He does. He just wants us to love and serve Him. Paul tells us in 1 Corinthians 2:9, "That is what the Scriptures mean when they say, 'No eye has seen, no ear has heard, and no mind has imagined what God has prepared for those who love him.'" We who are set apart are always going to have to deal with people that are confined to their worldly mindsets, but it's not like it won't be worth it. Serving the God we serve makes it worth it.

Seeds

The Bible uses the word "seed" in a couple different ways. Jesus often used seeds to symbolize His followers and in the Bible seeds are a representation of feelings or mentalities planted in the hearts of people. Basically, everything we experience, hear, watch, or do plants seeds in our hearts. The definition of a seed is a flowering plant's unit of reproduction, <u>capable of developing into another such plant</u>. As disciples, we have to be careful of the seeds we allow to be planted into our hearts, and the seeds we plant in the hearts of others. The Bible tells us, "A troublemaker plants seeds of strife; gossip separates the best of friends" (Proverbs 16:28). It's all about our influence. What are we allowing to be reproduced in our school, at our job, in our life? I know that if I walk up to a girl and tell her that she is ugly, it will plant a seed of insecurity, however, if I tell that girl she is beautiful, it will plant a seed of confidence.

A lot of us are guilty of letting so many different factors plant seeds in our hearts and affect what we reproduce to other people. It can be shows we watch on Netflix, music we listen to, or people we hang out with. I remember watching season two of *13 Reasons Why* (which is a very powerful show in my opinion) and it was as if the favorite word of the writer was *the f-bomb*. And I noticed that after watching episode after episode, I wanted to proclaim, "F-bomb" when I felt necessary. Well, it's because I allowed the seed that said it was okay to be planted in my heart, which then created more of an opportunity for me to fight my flesh (which is not fun). High school comes along with so many bad seeds to be planted in our hearts, and you can tell that they are bad seeds because they feed your flesh. It's a struggle to block out all of the cuss words, secular music, earthly mindsets, etc., but it is in the word of God where we find the right seeds that feed our spirit.

In the *Purpose* chapter of this book, I explained that at one point I saw my purpose as small. The biggest reason for that is because I allowed so many people to plant that seed in my heart. My dad helped me realize that because when I told him how I was feeling he said, "Was that from God or did you allow that seed to be planted in your heart?" That's when I realized that this whole "seeds" concept was important. The seeds that I allowed had the ability to take my mind and heart away from what God's called me to do.

I mentioned that what we see has the power to plant seeds in our hearts as did *13 Reasons Why* in mine. The Bible says, "Your eye is like a lamp that provides light for your body. When your eye is healthy, your whole body is filled with light. But when it is unhealthy, your body is filled with darkness" (Luke 11:34). We cannot be a light in this world if we allow darkness to enter into our hearts. You cannot produce a sunflower with a tulip seed. I know it's a lot easier to kick back and relax watching your favorite show on Netflix than it is to study the Bible. That's part of what holds us back from serving God to our full potential. But, if we allow the word of God to plant seeds in our hearts, we can reproduce His light. If we allow *13 Reasons Why* to plant seeds in our hearts (nothing against the show, I love it but let's be real it can get you a little depressed), we can only reproduce what's earthly. The word of God outputs love, forgiveness, faithfulness, and thankfulness. Earthly things output comparison, depression, hate, and so many other things opposite from God. I'm not saying you gotta stop watching your favorite show, I am no one to judge, but we must guard our hearts. If whatever you allow to be planted in your heart causes you to forget who you are in Christ, get rid of it.

Just like a flower seed is inside a flower, our spiritual seeds are inside of us, and what's inside of us affects what's on the outside of us. In the Bible, Jesus exclaims, "You blind Pharisee! First wash the inside of the cup and the dish, and then the outside will become clean, too" (Matthew 23:26). He is referring to the bodies of the Pharisees when He says "the cup and the dish" because they were the type of people that presented themselves different from who they actually were. The Pharisees were the type of people that were so careful to make sure they looked good on the outside, but on the inside Jesus says they were "full of greed and self-indulgence!" Matthew 23:26 makes it clear that what's on the inside of us makes us who we are. That's why it is so important to be aware of the seeds permitted in our life. Our seeds determine what people will see in us, just like a plant's seed does. That is why Jesus says, "*First*, wash the inside of the cup and dish, and *then* the outside will become clean, too." The spirits of the Pharisees were not right because the spirits within them were not from God. On the inside they were dirty, they just didn't let anyone see. It can be tempting to just put on a show because we are desperate for people to see us as one of the good ones or as holy, but just like the Pharisees, we can't hide our true spirits forever.

We can never have the right spirit if we don't have the right seeds. To make this clearer, I feel differently when I listen to secular music than I do when I listen to worship music. It's because secular music plants seeds in my heart from non Christ-like artists that give me a spirit similar to theirs, while worship music plants seeds in my heart from artists filled with the spirit of God that give me a spirit similar to Christ's. Which do you think is better? Now, I'm not throwing shots at any secular music because, of course, not all of it is bad, however, it's just not from God.

We do also have to be careful about how we receive seeds from God because there are differences. Jesus tells a parable about a farmer scattering seeds that fall on four different locations: a footpath, shallow soil, thorns, and fertile soil (Matthew 13: 3-8). He explains in verses 18-23:

> Now listen to the explanation of the parable about the farmer planting seeds: The seed that fell on the footpath represents those who hear the message about the Kingdom and don't understand it. Then the evil one comes and snatched away the seed that was planted in their hearts. The seed on the rocky soil represents those who hear the message and immediately receive it with joy. But since they don't have deep roots, they don't last

long. They fall away as soon as they have problems or are persecuted for believing God's word. The seed that fell among the thorns represents those who hear God's word, but all too quickly the message is crowded out but the worries of life and the lure of wealth, so no fruit is produced. The seed that fell on good soil represents those who truly hear and understand God's word and produce harvest of thirty, sixty, or even a hundred times as much as had been planted!

It can be easy to receive seeds on the footpath when we study the latest trends, song lyrics, and tv shows more than the word of God. It can be easy to receive seeds on the rocky soil when we get discouraged by the smallest setbacks or made fun of for our Christ-like mentalities. It can be easy to receive seeds on the thorns when we start worrying about what people will think if we're different. But, what's easy isn't worth fighting for! I pray that all of us young disciples in the world can learn to receive seeds on good, fertile soil, because what we can reproduce is far greater than us. Yes, adults can do it too, but how many teenagers do you know that like to listen to adults? To wrap all of this up, fellow disciples, in the name of Jesus, DO NOT allow worldly seeds that may be planted in your heart alter who you are and what God has called you to do. Also, be a disciple that plants seeds from God in the hearts of others and one that receives seeds on soil that will harvest a hundred times more!

Friends

There are multiple things that define a friendship. People see a "friend" in so many different ways. Some may believe that if you tell a friend that her shirt doesn't look cute, you're a good one. Others may believe that you're a sucky friend for saying such a thing.

Friends (after Christ and family) are the people that you walk through life with. They're the people you call when you wanna get something to eat, go shopping, play basketball, or just need somebody to talk to. If you're lucky, you may have that one friend that you would give your right arm to if they needed it because y'all are just there for each other like that. Jesus, who is the perfect example of a friend, tells us, "Greater love has no one then this: to lay down one's life for one's friends" (John 15:13). The day I first read this verse, I stopped and asked myself, "Would I die for the people I call my friends?" There were a couple to which the answer was yes and I realized that they were the ones that were similar to me. They were also living for Christ, and in my mind, that made them worthy. I was wrong. None of us are worthy of Jesus dying on the cross for us, so who was I to be the judge?

In high school, finding Christ-following friends can be so hard. Yeah, you got those kids that go to church and say that they're Christians, but deep down they haven't been reborn. Many believe in Christ, but few act like it. It's devastating because as teens we want somebody to hang out with or talk to when we're feeling lonely. But, because we are disciples of Christ, they can't just be anybody up in the school. I've learned the hard way that you can't call up your friend that doesn't really know Jesus if you're struggling in your faith, need Godly advice on a relationship, or advice on what to do when somebody does you wrong. They won't think, "What would Jesus do?" They will give you the answer your flesh wants, an answer based off of their feelings, not their faith. This is why we must be careful choosing the people we call "friends." The Bible tells us, "Do not be misled: 'Bad company corrupts good character'" (1 Corinthians 15:33).

Don't think for a second that I'm oblivious to the fact that some friends are just not that easy to drop. They've either been physically there for many years or you just don't want to deal with what comes after. I've been there. The problem with most unequally yoked friends is that they won't really understand you. They have another outlook on life that's hard to intertwine with yours. Some might say, "Well why don't you just get your non-saved friends saved?" Well, it's not that easy. Everyone knows that high school comes along with peer pressure, identity confusion, fear of not being accepted, etc. And it's not that easy to convince a teenager that's theoretically just trying to make it through all of the battles and fit in to believe, trust, and live for someone they do not see. Most kids just want what they do see.

Being unequally yoked with a friend who has no desire to be equally yoked will lead to a fool's friendship: it looks like friendship, it feels like friendship, but when you put it under pressure, they are not really your friend.

I know that not all of the people that you may be friends with, who are not saved, are bad people and won't be good to you. I have a few of those friends, and all we can do is pray for them. Maybe God just wants them to be around our spirit. However, we must really be careful and listen to the Holy Spirit on that subject because the Bible tells us, "Do not be yoked together with unbelievers. For what do righteousness and wickedness have in common? Or what fellowship can light have with darkness?" (2 Corinthians 6:14). If you feel your spirit darken around a certain person, they are not your friend. Stay away and get to praying away. There are just some people we have to love from a distance because you never know if the enemy will use that person to rock your foundation in Christ. From my experience, friendships with unequally yoked people will lead to a lot of disappointments. With the spirit of Christ in you, you will love harder and some people just won't know how to love and be the kind of friend you need them to be. How could they? They don't know Jesus - the perfect friend. Any relationship is a roller coaster, just make sure God wants you to get on the ride. I want to make it clear that just because somebody doesn't know God doesn't mean we shouldn't associate with them at all. After all, they are the ones we are supposed to be reaching.

Friendships in high school (especially with girls) can get pretty complicated. It's like, as a follower of Christ, you don't want to have bad blood with anybody, but let's say you're friends with a girl and she doesn't like this other girl you're friends with so she tries to talk about her to you. Then, you're stuck between defending the other girl or keeping the peace with the friend you are talking to at the moment. If you've ever been in this situation, you know that the next move isn't that simple. Of course the right thing to do is stop the girl from talking about your other friend, but how many know that it's almost like peer pressure? Before you know it, you start agreeing with the girl! I am guilty of falling into this trap and actually thought it was okay once. I felt that it was harmless since we were only talking to each other and the other girl never had to know. Jesus tells us, "And I tell you this, you must give an account on judgement day for every idle word you speak" (Matthew 12:36), and that helped me realize that the words I chose to agree with actually had some harm. Representing Christ is way more important than pleasing a "friend" at any moment. I know it's hard and I am plenty guilty of just trying to keep the peace with everyone. Don't get me wrong, your relationship with most people can still be peaceful (if you respond the right way), but as disciples we cannot let other people, especially the ones we call "friend," influence who we are. If they're your friends, they are mostly likely going to plant many seeds in your heart. Make sure you are careful to not allow certain ones to be reproduced as a result of you wanting to please people and not be left out of your favorite clique.

Finding God-fearing friends in high school isn't exactly the easiest thing to do in life, but it's something worth fighting for. It is necessary. The few that I have are amazing and I love them dearly. Godly friends are the friends that will hold you accountable and vice versa. Another benefit is that you get to learn from them as well. Each of us have areas in our life that are not so squeaky clean, but just imagine having a friend with the spirit of Christ that God uses to help guide you, love you, and push you towards your purpose. Your God-fearing friends will fail you too sometimes, nobody is perfect, and everyone has a sinful nature. But, if your relationship is truly led by God, you will reconcile and get back on track. God doesn't want us to feel alone, even Jesus had a circle of friends that He had to work with to keep the relationship. The Bible even tells us, "The Lord God said, 'It is not good for the man to be alone. I will make a helper suitable for him.'" (Genesis 2:18). If we were meant to be alone, God would've never created Eve for Adam; however, be aware of who you let in the garden. Hey, ya never know, maybe we could be friends. ;)

FOMO
(Fear of Missing Out)

In life, nobody wants to be left out of anything. It hurts when people hang out and don't invite you. You feel like you're missing out on all the fun. This fear of missing out sometimes blinds us from knowing what God's will is. What if God didn't want you at the specific place your friends were going to? You might ask, "Well, how do I know if God wants me to go to this certain place, or do this certain thing or not?" Paul tells us in Romans 12:2 "Do not conform to the pattern of this world but be transformed by the renewing of your mind. Then you will be able to test and approve what God's will is - His good, pleasing, and perfect will." The pattern of the high school world is that if you don't hang out with people or go have fun when everyone else does or HOW everyone else does, they are better than you. It might go unspoken, but basically you are labeled as "lame." It's in our nature as teenagers to want to conform to the pattern to avoid being belittled. I know a common problem for boys is that in most male high school cliques, the amount of sex you have with girls is a factor in determining your worth. So, I know that as a guy, you may start to fear that you're missing out on all the pleasure of sex with girls before marriage because of how much belittling you are subjected to each day. Girls can have the same problem as well. I remember sitting in a classroom at school and I started looking through the pages of my friend's anatomy book.

47

There were a couple other friends around us and I came across the page with the anatomy of a penis on it. For giggles, I acted like I was studying it. Everyone around me knew my purity stance because of my love for Christ and I assume with intentions to make fun of me, my friend laughingly says, "Alexis, are you confused?" I played it off, but I knew that she basically just wanted to joke about the fact that I hadn't had sex. The devil will speak through other people like this to try to make us feel like the decisions we make (because of our love for Christ) are not worth anything. He wants us to believe that things are so much better on the other side. But, because my mind is renewed, I know what God's will for my purity is. You won't be in bondage with the fear of missing out if you already know that God has things in store that are greater than the things that people want you to believe you're missing out on.

Sometimes, we find ourselves in situations to which we really don't know if we should be in. We just agree to something in the spur of the moment because not only do we have the fear of missing out, but also the fear that we will be judged if we say "no." It's at times like this when we have to ask ourselves the same question Paul asked himself in Galatians 1:10, "Am I now trying to win the approval of human beings, or of God? Or am I trying to please people? If I were trying to please people, I would not be a servant of Christ." To make this simpler: The curiosity you may have one day about what's going to happen at a party, may stop you from having the opportunity to do something for Christ's kingdom. I'm not saying that God won't ever tell you to go to a party

48

to pray for somebody or something, but if you do things out of fear of missing out on what the world has to offer, you may miss what God has already provided.

Matthew 6:21 says, "For where your treasure is, there your heart will be also." Treasure can be defined as "something valuable," therefore, if doing what everybody else is doing all the time is valuable to us, the Bible says that's where our heart will be. Our heart is a special place because it controls everything. We fall in love with people in our hearts, when we are hurt we feel it in our hearts, when we are happy we feel it in our hearts, and just like the two men on the day that Jesus rose from the dead, when we are in the presence of God, we feel it in our hearts. We fear in our hearts as well. We'll talk more about fear in a later chapter, but what we need to understand now is that if we have the fear of missing out on the teenage dream in our hearts, it's hard for us to receive Jesus in our hearts. To prove it: 1 John 4:18 says, "There is no fear in love. But perfect love drives out fear, because fear has to do with punishment. The one who fears is not made perfect in love." Jesus IS perfect love, and the Bible says that He drives out fear, therefore, if we fear such things, do we really have Jesus? I know that it's hard because we all have a flesh that fears missing out on things and wants to know what it's like to do certain things. Our spirit cannot get pulled into that because then Jesus will no longer be our treasure.

In the world, you'll always be wondering "what if," but if the word of God is your treasure, you will know what is to come. I'm not saying God is going to tell you every single thing that will happen in the future, but, for example, you won't wonder "What if I meet a guy/girl if I go to this place?" because you will already know God has somebody out there for you that He will send when you're ready.

It's extremely easy to be influenced in high school. People will manipulate you into believing that you aren't as important or worthy as they are, hence making you feel like you have something to prove. Sometimes, we can get caught up in the fear of missing out on what other people have instead of being thankful for our portion. We all know that there's just certain people in our high school whom everyone else wants to be because of what they have. It tricks us into believing that what we have is more important than who we are. Jesus is talking to His disciples when He says, "And what do you benefit if you gain the whole world but lose your own soul? Is anything worth more than your soul?" (Matthew 16:26). In my walk with Christ, I've had to realize that, no, I might not be the most popular, but God knows my name and He calls me His. I might not have the most money, but the God that owns everything provides for me. I might not be who other people want me to be, but God has a purpose for who I am!

When you follow Christ, the only thing you'll miss out on is emptiness. Yeah, what this world offers can look appetizing sometimes, but in the Bible, James proclaims, "You adulterers! Don't you realize that friendship with the world makes you an enemy of God? I say it again: If you want to be a friend of the world, you make yourself an enemy of God" (James 4:4). I don't know about you, but I love God and don't want to be His enemy, therefore, I choose to follow what He says is great, not what the world says is great.

I know people will mock you if you don't do what they do or act how they act. I know they will see you as less than because you're "missing out" on the teenage dream, but Jesus tells us, "Be happy about it! Be very glad! For a great reward awaits you in heaven. And remember, the ancient prophets were persecuted in the same way" (Matthew 5:12). Don't have a fear of missing out, have joy that you have what everyone needs: the presence of God. With God, you will endure way more than what you'll "miss out" on. In Jesus' name!

Social Media

Social media is a fun, yet dangerous platform in our generation. It's the stage that everyone performs on to get people to see the version of themselves they want seen. It's a wall that we sometimes hide behind to cover up the fact that we're not perfect. It's like, "Oh, I'm not feeling so emotionally great today, but I can't let everyone else know that, so I'll post a selfie!" Of course this is not the case for everyone, but it's hard to find a teenage girl in high school that is not defined by her Instagram likes. I've actually known kids (boys and girls) who have deleted pictures because they didn't get as many likes as they wanted. Social media actually allows us to really rely on the acceptance of others. That's why as followers of Christ, it's critical for us to guard our hearts. Social media is cool and all, but in reality, God would want us to use it, with all its "coolness," to reach the ones that hide behind the wall. I'm not saying that every post you make must have a Bible verse in it. Everyone has a life, and sometimes it's okay if we just want to humbly share it, however, our main purpose in life is to share the gospel. So, if our peers spend most of their time on social media, what better way to fulfill our purpose?

Social media creates a way for people to send messages to people without actually talking to them. On Twitter it's known as "subtweet." Twitter is the social media that you can use to post whatever is on your mind without actual confrontation. I enjoy Twitter because on it you can find inspirational tweets and tweets about things that you didn't know anyone else related to. But sometimes we can get caught up in posting a lot of our feelings on Twitter (or any social media). It causes us to cast our cares on whichever social media forum rather than casting our cares on the Lord. I had this friend, who was a follower of Christ, and every time she felt something new or found out something new about her ex-boyfriend she would tweet about it instead of taking all her feelings and concerns to God. She ended up regretting it because she was going to the wrong place for her healing and actually wondered why she was still hurting.

Most of us check our social media when we're bored or just relaxing. As teenagers, it just becomes a big part of our lives whether we realize it or not. A lot of times it's the first thing we look at the in morning and the last thing we see at night. I'm guilty of it. There have been plenty of times when I've been hurt by something I've seen on social media, yet I continue to engage in it every day.

Mostly all social medias have different purposes. There's Facebook, which in my experience is more enjoyed by adults. Facebook is the social media we typically use to keep up with our families, tell people "happy birthday," and see into the evolving lives of other people. Next, we have Snapchat, which is typically the main source of communication in our generation. It's also what we use to show people what we're doing at certain times, how good we look on certain days, and how great of a life we have. Then, again, we have Twitter where we share what's on our minds, how we're feeling, or inspiration.

Finally, we have Instagram where we post selfies, pics from important times in our lives, and pics that make us stunt on people. All the main social medias include us saying words, whether it's the entire post or just a caption on a picture. We don't necessarily have to answer the words we say on social media (unless it's cyber bullying or suicidal). The words we type can be empty, meaningless, inspiring, full of life, dark, or actually have meaning. I know that when I make a post on any social media, the words I choose to let whoever follows me read matters because Jesus tells us, "The words you say will either acquit you or condemn you" (Matthew 12:37). That is why I encourage all of us followers of Christ to be a light on social media. There are boys and girls that get all kinds of seeds planted in their hearts that do not point them towards Jesus. Like I explained in the "purpose" chapter, we are called to plant the right seeds. Teenagers compare themselves to posts they see every day, but what if they saw your post that says, "God loves you just the way you are." And don't post it for the likes, the shares, the retweets, etc. Post it because there are people out there that need to hear more of the gospel and see the love of God. Paul didn't get no retweets. It's up to us to turn what the devil likes to use for destruction into something that God can reach His children through. Social media should know the name "Jesus."

We All Want Love

Love, Love, Love... who doesn't want it? True love is something that people chase after their entire lives. The sad part is they never encounter God's love. In the Bible, John tells us a little bit about love saying, "Dear friends, let us love one another, for love comes from God. Everyone who loves has been born of God and knows God. Whoever does not love does not know God because God is love. This is how God showed His love among us: "He sent his one and only son into the world that we might live through him" (1 John 4:7-9). John basically tells us that if we don't know God, we will never fully understand the concept of love, because God IS love. People often believe that if they find true love, they will have everything they need. They're right... except for the fact that they believe they will find it here on Earth. Love *is* all we need and who is love?

True love is one of the desires of our hearts at such a young age. I was actually baffled when I was a little girl in my third-grade class, and a friend of mine told me that she had a boyfriend. Of course, as nine-year-old's, we did not know what having a boyfriend really meant, what it really meant when we said we "loved" them, and what the purpose of all of it was. Growing up, we just knew that having a boyfriend was cool, and that deep down we longed for it. It's not like it controlled our lives or anything, but somehow, we felt like we were less important if we didn't have a boyfriend. I was just a little bit of a tomboy while growing up so I kind of kept my heart's desires on the down low. I was actually friends with a lot of guys in elementary school, and I feel like they allowed it because I wasn't chasing after them like the rest of the females. I did have my crushes though. ;)

In middle school, the game changed. Not only did you have a boyfriend, but you also talked to them outside of school whether by phone or (if you were lucky) hanging out. I think it's safe to say that boys were never really my focus in middle school, but I still would've probably jumped at the opportunity to have a suitable boyfriend. It's not like I thought it was that serious, but it still somehow dictated our lives and was hard to ignore. If not already in elementary school, middle school is when everyone was getting their first kiss, and when having a companion just seemed like the most important thing in the world.

The game alters even more in high school. Every hall you walk down and every corner you turn, there's a couple boo'd up with each other. If you're just one of the ordinary, single kids, it may disgust you, but let's admit that most of the time we think, "I want that." It feels crazy to actually admit that I was looking for love at such a young age. It's embarrassing, but so were the other girls throughout the school. It's not like most of the couples actually knew what love was, but I still desired a connection with someone. As girls, we want to feel wanted, loved, and valued. I can't really speak for guys, but in most cases, getting a boyfriend or girlfriend is a main goal in high school. We think a companion is going to fill the hole inside of us. It's another thing the world likes to use to define our worth. Demi Lovato said it best singing,

"You ain't nobody 'til you got somebody!" in her hit song *Tell Me You Love Me*. They may not say it out loud, but a lot of kids believe it... I sure did for a brief minute. Most of my friends had had boyfriends or currently had one at the time, and I had never got the chance to experience it. I knew that God was love and that He was supposed to be filling the void in my heart, but I was always insecure about it. My friends would always say, "We gotta find you a boyfriend," and although their intentions were harmless, they were basically implying that having a boyfriend would complete me. I always shrugged it off, but deep down, it just kept making me more insecure. Somedays, I would reason with myself and think, "Number one: I lowkey would not really know how to act around a guy that I liked. Number two: I was insecure of what people would think if I had a boyfriend. And number three: I didn't even really like any of the guys at my school." However, there was always a part of me that wanted somebody on this Earth to love, to go out on dates with, and to just have the normal high school dating relationship with. I wrote in my journal on May 14, 2016 (I was 15 years old): "I kinda feel terrible. I'm depressed. Nothing in my life is special. I feel like the answer is to read my Bible, but still. I know it's dumb, but I'm very insecure about not having a boyfriend or even talking to a guy. I just want to feel pretty, but I don't..." I feel like God knew that I wouldn't be who He called me to be if I continued to desire love from someone other than Him, and in turn, be insecure and depressed because of it; therefore, on May 17, 2017, He gave me what I wanted: I started talking to a boy.

I was sixteen and at the end of the second semester of my sophomore year. I can't remember if it was the day before or two days before I started talking to him, but one day in my English class, my friend pulls me aside all giggly-like and says, "I know somebody that has the feels for you." I was honestly in shock and denial as soon as she said it, and I doubtfully asked, "Who?" She replied, "Now, before I tell you, you have to promise to give it a chance." At this point I am really doubtful and assume that it is no one I will be attracted to and someone I've known for a while. I look at her questionably and say, "Okay, just tell me who it is." Now, for privacy purposes, let's just call him "Adam" (which literally means "the man" in Hebrew). My friend finally told me the man's name and my first response was "Who the heck is Adam?" It turned out that Adam had been in my Adv. Algebra/Trigonometry class the entire semester and was a senior (why I didn't really know him). My friend knew that he liked me because Adam was actually friends with the guy she was talking to. It had been a year since I wrote the depressing note in my journal, and at that point I had drawn closer to God and was identifying with who I was in Him. I feel like it's safe to say that I no longer felt like I needed a guy to be worthy, and maybe that's why God sent Adam. *shrugs* Well, after my friend told me about Adam, I could not stop thinking about it for the rest of the class and was SO SCARED to go to the next period (Adv. Algebra/Trig.). I did, however, have a little advantage: I sat in the back of the class and Adam was at the front. I'll admit, I sometimes stared at the back of his head like a creepy, stalker woman. I believe it was the next day when

58

my friend whispered in my ear, "Somebody's gonna Snapchat you today." It was after school on a Wednesday when I got the Snapchat that said, "Hey," and boy were his eyes beautiful. We talked and got to know each other up until I went to church that night. I was SO NERVOUS to see him the next day at school. I didn't know if he was gonna talk to me when people were around or if we were just gonna keep our thing on the downlow... I just didn't know! Well, the next day came and I was sitting in the math class working on class work when a deep voice startled me and said, "Can you check to see if these are right?" I managed to not make a fool of myself while I helped him with his work, even though I was freaking out on the inside. The rest of the school year (which was only a few days...maybe a week) involved numerous Snapchats back and forth and occasional talks in person...more like two. I sought God more than ever in that period because I knew that I did not want to get deep into a relationship if it wasn't God's will for my life at the time. After days of talking, Adam got the courage to ask me out on a date. I bravely said "yes" without even talking to my mom and dad about it. In all honesty, the only opinion I cared about was God's because I had seen many of my friends get heartbroken over a guy and I wanted God to tell me if the same thing was going to happen to me. At the time it felt like God was silent, yet in my mind I didn't hear a "no." Looking back, I feel like the Holy Spirit was like, "If you want to experience this, go for it. If not, it's cool." After the talk with my mom and dramatization with my dad, I went on my first date with Adam to the movies. Pushing past all the nervousness, we had a good time. We sat outside after the movie was over in hope that the rain would slow down, because as a black girl, my hair and I are not about that rain life. It was in those few minutes that I became a girlfriend, and I remember thinking, "I could totally fall in love with this kid."

The summer was filled with dates, talks, iMessage games, and good times. It was all a dream... until it wasn't. After getting comfortable with Adam, his true colors were revealed. He wasn't at all a bad person, but not exactly the Christ-like boyfriend I'd always wanted. Our great talks and awesome dates turned into bickering and dates that included arguing and regret. By the end of the summer, I was over having a boyfriend. I often said, "I miss the old Adam" because I felt like he wasn't putting in as much effort as he was when he was trying to win me. If you're a guy reading this right now: Never stop chasing! Once you have her, still work to keep her. By the time school started back, I was on the verge of breaking up with Adam. I feel bad for admitting this, but I honestly thought about staying with Adam until PROM so I wouldn't have to worry about getting a date. Crazy, rude, and selfish? I know. I did not carry out that plan because I honestly couldn't take it anymore. You would think that a break-up after a two-month relationship wouldn't be that bad, but boy was this guy HOOKED. I mean like he was trying to tell me that he loved me and all that and I straight up did not feel the same. I don't know if God just felt like my season with Adam needed to end or what because out of all the things he said to try to keep me, my heart just would not let him in again. It wasn't like the break up was easy for me, but I only felt bad because of how much it was hurting Adam. He hadn't done anything bad and drastic to me, he just wasn't for me.

So, you might be sitting there thinking, "So, uhh why did you tell us all of that girl? This book is supposed to be about God?" Well, the reason I shared this experience is because I know that there is at least one person out there that is feeling the same thing that I felt. You feel like somehow you are being cheated out of one of the best parts of being a teenager. In high school, heck, in life, we all want love, but if you're a young girl or boy in your teen years and you really want to get into a relationship because you're tired of being single, let me just tell you, it is not worth it. Now, I'm not saying that God won't ever go ahead and reveal someone's husband or wife to them in high school because He has different plans for us all. But, if you are led by your feelings rather than your faith, you and your boy or girlfriend will be the ones working to keep the relationship together, not God. Don't be afraid to put that boy or girl in the friend zone, after all, it is better than breaking their heart. In my relationship, it was obvious that God was no longer for it because Adam was the only one that wanted to stay in it. You might ask, "Well, why would God let you go through it in the first place if He knew it was gonna end?" The answer to that is because I learned. God let me experience what I thought I was missing out on to teach me. I learned that with Christ in my heart, I couldn't just give it away to just anyone, especially someone that didn't also have Christ in their heart. I mentioned in the "Identity" chapter that because our identity is in Christ and since he was a beautiful person, our spirits and personalities are beautiful. Adam didn't necessarily have a hard time letting go of me, he had a hard time letting go of the spirit within me. During that summer, I drew closer to God and started realizing who I was in Christ, therefore, in the image of a growing godly woman, I was expecting Adam to treat me as such, and be a godly man, when he was just a lost teenage boy. I do feel bad for not leading Adam towards God as much I should've, but towards the end, I knew he wasn't going to be my husband, so, I thought, "What the point?" and did not want to be around him. Don't be mistaken, it was not my job, nor is it yours, to change whoever you're interested in. There's a difference between leading someone to Christ in a friendly way and trying to change who they are for your benefit. I made that mistake with another guy that I met. He was everything Adam wasn't, but still wasn't saved. I thought I could mold him into the godly man I wanted him to grow up to be, but guess what? He was just a teenage boy and it wasn't my job to try to do what God would eventually do all because of my desire to be with him. My youth pastor describes it as "mission date." Mission dating is when we start dating someone because we like them and try to change their heart along the way. Our boyfriend or girlfriend becomes a project. Listen, only God can change someone's heart. And girls, the man is supposed to water YOU with the word of God, not the other way around. I told Adam, "Go get you a Bible and a relationship with God, then we can talk." If they go to church with you just to get closer to you, they are going for the wrong reason. Their relationship with God should not be dependent on you. The desires has to be in THEIR own heart. You can love them from afar, just don't give them your heart without their heart belonging to Christ. They won't know how to properly love you, and if it's a guy, they won't know how to properly lead you. In the Bible, the bride in Song of Solomon 2:7 says, "Daughters of Jerusalem, I charge you by the gazelles and by the does of the field: Do not arouse or awaken love until it so desires." I wish I would've just waited much longer for God to show me the only person I was supposed to open my heart to, but I'm also thankful for the experience and everything that I learned. He knows what He's doing because if it wasn't for my experience, I couldn't sit here and encourage all of you about something that I could relate to. I learned not only from my mistakes, but from the mistakes that my friends made all the times they dated guys. I am now on track to become the woman God wants me to be, before He sends the man that will not complete me, but intensify the ministry that God puts before me. In the end, glorifying God is all that matters. If done right, the person you marry will be the person that God made specifically for you. Notice that I said, "If done right" because as soon as we start letting our feelings lead us, we end up married to someone we don't really love with the child we've always wanted, just with the wrong person. But, if both of you are led by your spirit, nothing or no one can get in the way of you and your God-sent boo. A great example in the Bible is the story of Isaac and Rebekah (Genesis 24): Abraham, Isaac's father, sent his senior servant to his home country to find a wife for Isaac. When the servant got to the country, he arrived at a spring and prayed to God that when the women came out to draw water, and he asked one of them for a drink, that the one that was for Isaac would also offer to give water to his camels. Rebekah was the one that gave the servant and his camels something to drink. The servant praised God and asked Rebekah to spend the night with her family at her house. The servant arrived at Rebekah's house and told her brother, Laban, and her father, Bethuel, his mission and his prayer to the Lord. He finally asked them if Rebekah would be able to leave with him to marry Isaac. "Laban and Bethuel answered, 'This is from the Lord; we can say nothing to you one way or the other'" (Genesis 24:50). Even they knew that if God made Isaac and Rebekah for each other, they couldn't do anything about it.

I know that as teenagers, we have a while before we'll get married to the love of our life, but I know (and I can only speak for females) that it's on our minds often. In fear, my friend asked me one day, "What if you never find a husband?" and I told her, "I'm not really worried about it." I know that if I'm walking in purpose and being who God called me to be, when the time is right, he'll send the Adam that I'm supposed to be with. And the same goes for you as well. So, I encourage all of us young people to not try to rush love. From all the experiences I've seen, it ends in disaster. Instead, girls, wait for the man that will want you as much as Jacob wanted Rachel. In the Bible, Genesis 29:20 tells us, "So Jacob served seven years to get Rachel, but they seemed like only a few days to him because of his love for her." And guys, wait for the woman that will show kindness and only seek your attention as Ruth did to Boaz. In the Bible, Ruth 3:10 says, "'The Lord bless you, my daughter.' he replied. 'This kindness is greater than that which you showed earlier. You have not run after the younger men, whether rich or poor.'" Ruth was so kind to Boaz and showed that she was down for only him.

Love and marriage are beautiful things. If God didn't think it was important, He never would have made the woman out of the man. In the Bible, Genesis 2:24 tells us, "That is why a man leaves his father and mother and is united to his wife, and they become one flesh." I was watching another one of Heather Lindsey's YouTube videos one day, and what really spoke to me is when she said that marriage was ministry. I thought, "I wouldn't want to be in ministry for the Lord with just anybody." She also said that we must ask ourselves, "If it doesn't have a purpose, why am I in it?" That goes for just normal relationships before marriage as well, because if the ultimate goal is not marriage and it doesn't bring glory to God, what's the point? I know that high school is typically the time when us teens experiment, have fun, and just date guys and girls when the flesh wants us to, but, none of that will draw us closer to Christ and lead us to our purpose. Of course there is absolutely nothing wrong with having fun, but we just must make sure that God would approve of the context in which we are doing it. I'm also not saying, "Oh stay away from the opposite sex until you're grown." I'm just saying that whether it's a friendship or relationship, make sure it has meaning. I've seen too many hearts get broken over meaningless relationships that didn't have the love of God in the middle (including my own). We all want love, but the love of God must be enough before anyone else's will... especially in high school.

Purity

Okay, let me just start off by saying that hormones are crazy! Now, our bodies are special objects that were initially created from dust, so of course God wants us to honor Him with them. When I think of the word "pure," I think of something being in the state in which it was created. If you have pure tea, that means that nothing (such as sugar, honey, or milk) has come in contact with it to alter how it was when I was originally created. God ultimately wanted us to stay in the same state He created us in: without sin, but thanks to Adam and Eve, we failed him early on. He did, however, send His son to die on the cross for our sins, but our sinful nature keeps us far from God. In the Bible, Galatians 5:19-21 tells us, "When you follow the desires of your sinful nature, the results are very clear: sexual immorality, impurity, lustful pleasures, idolatry, sorcery, hostility, quarreling, jealousy, outbursts of anger, selfish ambition, dissension, division, envy, drunkenness, wild parties, and other sins like these. Let me tell you again, as I have before, that anyone living that sort of life will not inherit the Kingdom of God." That pretty long list is a big part of what can keep us impure. It's not how we were originally created because the Word says we were created in the image of God. So how do we get so messed up sometimes? I personally blame our ragging teenage hormones. Just kidding…kinda. In this life, we are born into sin, but God still wants us to honor and represent him in every way possible.

This isn't the coolest or easiest subject to talk about. Purity seems so lame in the eyes of so many teenagers, especially if you have a boyfriend or girlfriend. In this society, sex (and other sexual practices) has become something casual. Through the years, people have downplayed the fact that God intended it for marriage. Sex is powerful. It's an intimacy that's not supposed to be shared with just anyone. Sex was God's idea. God has called each of us to do so many great things, not be on the show *16 and Pregnant*. We talked in the "Young" chapter about how this is the time when we build the foundation of our future, not slow down the progress of it. We are all brothers and sisters, so I don't want you to feel like I'm lecturing you, but I do think it's important that I say what God put on my heart about this subject because it's become a big part of our world in this generation. There are young people that still take part in living their best life after getting pregnant young, but that's all because of the grace of mercy of our God. In the Bible, Paul wrote to the young pastor Timothy saying, "Don't let anyone think less of you because you are young. Be an example to all believers in what you say, in the way you live, in your love, your faith, and your **purity**" (1 Timothy 4:12). Our purity is important to God, especially when we're young. Now, when we get married, that's when we're supposed to get lit. I made the decision to remain pure until marriage when I was 12 years old. I knew that sex was something that I only wanted to have with the one whom I would spend the rest of my life with. If I said that to most of the people in my high school, they would probably either laugh or think I was dramatic. When I was young, I saw the older cousin I looked up to get hurt so many times because she gave her boyfriends the benefit of a husband when they didn't intend on making her a wife. Most of society tells us that there's nothing wrong with have premature sex, but as children of God, we have to cling to what the word of God says. I asked a girl that had just told me that she had been intimate with her boyfriend, "What if he's not your husband?" And she said, "Then he's not." It honestly broke my heart because she had just given a part of herself to someone she may not even know in a few years.

Sex outside of marriage has the power to create broken families. For example, my father got a woman pregnant with my brother, and then two years later, got my mother pregnant with me. They each gave a part of themselves to my dad, without even fully having him. The sex they chose to have when they were young led to a broken family, broken hearts, and three kids by two women for my dad. He's saved now and owns up to his mistakes, but he says all the time that he wishes he would have waited and did it God's way. In the Bible, King Solomon, the wisest man, says, "Drink water from your own well, share your love only with your wife. Why spill the water of your springs in the streets, having sex with just anyone? You should reserve it for yourselves. Never share it with strangers." Girls, if your earthly father, perhaps, gave you a watch, when you were young, to give to your future husband, would you just give pieces of that watch to every guy you dated? Boys, if your mother gave you a ring, when you were young, to give to your future wife, would you just give diamonds from the rings to every girl you dated? I noticed in my two-month relationship that I talked about in the last chapter, that I really had to be careful with how intimate I got with "Adam." We would kiss and it would be great. At one point, I thought I was in love with him, but, I just had lust for him. You see, that's a huge reason why our purity before marriage is such a big deal to God. He wants us to fall in love with the soul He made for us, not with the lips and body of another person's husband or wife. They may be fine, but if God didn't send them, it's a waste of time. Don't confuse lust with love, because you can't enhance and minister into the kingdom of God on a foundation of lust. My lust for "Adam" felt good in the moment, but God said, "What about forever?"

God of course loves us whether we are "pure" or not, but I just want to encourage us young disciples to submit and do it God's way. The reward is so much greater. I understand that there's people out there who's choice was taken away from them. I understand that there's people out there who didn't know any better before they knew Christ, or don't know any better now. I'm not at all saying that people who save sex for marriage are worth more than people who don't or don't know to. Jesus made us all pure by dying on the cross for our sins. I love God, therefore, I'm going to do my best to honor Him with my body, my heart, and my mind. I pray you'll do the same, because this world needs it.

In the Bible, Proverbs 31:25 talks about the Wife of Noble Character saying, "She is clothed with strength and dignity, she can laugh at the days to come." To all my girls, we are a treasure to be found and a prize to be won. Don't lose your strength when the wrong Adam comes along, and don't lose your dignity when he wants to seduce you before securing his heart with you. To all the guys, be patient. Don't take a piece of her without giving her all of you.

Love, Peace, and Purity ☺

Fear

Fear is something that is inevitably a struggle for everyone. We all are afraid of something whether we like it or not. Fear is a tricky subject because 2 Timothy 1:7 tells us, "For God has not given us a spirit of fear and timidity, but of power, love, and self-discipline." In life, I know that God doesn't want me to fear anything but living in this world makes it hard not to. When I was young, I always heard people in church say that they, "Fear God," and it made me confused because I was under the impression that God was loving. I remember thinking, "Would God hurt us?" I was sixteen years old when I came across Heather Lindsey's YouTube video called *What it Means to Fear God*. In this video, she taught that there are two types of fear: Fear of the Lord and Fear of the Spirit of Fear. From her teaching, I learned that the "Fear of the Lord" was more of just respect for God. It's the same thing as loving your mother, therefore, respecting her and being fearful when she's upset with you. Heather Lindsey explained the fear of the Lord as, "Because of my fear of the Lord, I won't sin, and I respect you," and she explained the fear of the spirt of fear as "afraid of things not working out." After her video, it was pretty clear to me that the "Fear of the Lord" was the only fear God wants us to have.

A fear I once had was the fear that things wouldn't always turn out the way that I wanted them to. I wanted everything done MY way. In the growth of my relationship with Christ, I had to realize that God was in control. It didn't matter how hard I worked to get what I wanted, or how much I begged my mom for something. I soon found out that if it wasn't God's will, it wasn't happening. That used to scare me, because just like an obnoxious teenager, I felt like I knew what was best for me and that if things didn't happen the way I wanted them to, they would fail. In the Bible, the Teacher tells us, "Accept the way God does things, for who can straighten what he has made crooked?" (Ecclesiastes 7:13). God knows everything that is going to happen before we even open our eyes in the morning. He knows every outcome of every possibility in every situation, and only does things for our good, but somehow fear influences us to want to change the way God does things because we're scared of the outcome. For example: My aunt was in her thirties when she got married, and the only reason she got married when she had the opportunity to is because she was scared that she would never get the chance again. Instead of accepting the fact that God was making her wait to either mold her or her intended husband into the woman or man they needed to be for marriage, she made the decision to change the plan for her life. (Exclusive: It wasn't worth it.) Yes, there can be fear when put your life in someone else's hands, but we must realize and understand, before it's too late, that God being in control is GOOD. Don't be afraid to not get into the college you want, because guess what if it's God's will and you do your part, it will happen. Fear creates friction in our walk with God and stops us from being the best version of the man/woman that God created us to be. I rebuke all fear right now in the name of Jesus!

Fear is basically the absence of faith. The definition of faith is "the complete trust or confidence in someone or something." We all know that our faith is in God, but there have been times when I felt like my fear was overshadowing my faith. At those times, I knew God and I knew I was supposed to trust Him, but I was still afraid of the things that I didn't know. In the Bible, Hebrews 11:6 tells us, "And without faith it is impossible to please God, because anyone who comes to him must believe that he exists and that he rewards those who earnestly seek him." It's crazy how such a little spirit as the spirit of fear has the power to make us forget about the spirit of God. For example, if you're walking down the street and a person with a knife jumps out at you, you're most likely going to be afraid. Your first thought probably won't be, "God is bigger than this," it'll be, "I'm going to die," or "How am I gonna get out of this situation?" When we become fearful of things other than God, situations come up and we think, "What am I gonna do?" The only reason we fear is because we rely on ourselves. When you try to make way for yourself in this life, yes, you will have a fear of things not going your way and failing. But, when you put your faith in God, such fears cease to exist. I used to fear that I would never find the right friends while I was still in high school. I was relying on myself to go out and find the people that God wanted me to share part of my life with, but once I started seeking Him only and trusting in Him, they were lead to me! Fear has no room in your heart when you're overwhelmed with the love of God. Like I mentioned earlier, "Perfect love casts out all fear" (1 John 4:18).

I also mentioned earlier that living in this world makes it hard not to fear, and it's true. It's a battle, as a teenage girl, to not fear things, such as, going to the grocery store alone at night, or the creepy old man that keeps smiling at me in the library that I'm writing this book in. It's hard as a high schooler to not worry about worldly things, such as, having some of the nicest clothes and shoes, or being known by the right people. Jesus tells us, "That is why I tell you not to worry about everyday life, whether you have enough food and drink, or enough clothes to wear. Isn't life more than food and your body more than clothing? Look at the birds. They don't plant or harvest or store food in barns for your heavenly Father feeds them. And aren't you far more valuable to him than they are? Can all your worries add a single moment to your life?" (Matthew 6: 25-27). Not only is fear irrelevant since God didn't give it to us, but in this scripture, Jesus practically tells us that it is pointless to fear. To make it clearer, if I went to the grocery store alone at night and I got into a situation that put my safety in jeopardy, the fear I would have of dying would not keep me alive, only the grace of God would. God takes care of the birds and the bees, so of course there's nothing to fear for you and me.

The number one reason most of us don't do or hesitate to do what God tells us to do is fear. We talked earlier about, in high school, the fear of what people will think about us if we are truly living the unashamed godly life. In the Bible, Moses initially didn't want to obey God and free the Israelites from Pharaoh. First, he had the fear of not being worthy: "But Moses said to God, 'Who am I that I should go to

Pharaoh and bring the Israelites out of Egypt?'" (Exodus 3:11). He was scared because, like most of us, he feared that he wasn't worthy enough to fulfill such a big calling as this. In reality, he wasn't (and we are not), BUT God said, "I will be with you…" (Exodus 3:12). Second, Moses allowed his fear to stir up his insecurities: "Moses said to the Lord, 'Pardon your servant, Lord. I have never been eloquent, neither in the past nor since you have spoken to your servant. I am slow of speech and tongue'" (Exodus 4:10). Like Moses, we let our fear allow us to hide behind our insecurities, BUT God said, "Who gave human beings their mouth? Who makes them deaf or mute? Who gives them sight or makes them blind? Is it not I, the Lord?" (Exodus 4:11). God is basically saying, "Bruh, did I not make you? And you wanna tell me what you can't do?!" That wasn't enough for Moses, and finally, he pleaded: "But Moses said, 'Pardon your servant, Lord. Please send someone else" (Exodus 4:13). His fear influenced him to ask the maker of heaven and earth not to use him to break people's shackles! Fear may be irrelevant, but it is powerful if we allow it. God is still the most powerful since, as we know, Moses did end up leading the Israelites out of Egypt, and he didn't even have to really work. All he had to do was tell Pharaoh what the Lord said, and if Pharaoh gave him trouble, God took care of it. Brothers and sisters, when God tells you to do something that's out of your comfort zone, do not let fear stop you. You may have battles along the way, but just like God said to the people of Judah and Jerusalem when they were under attack: "But you will not even need to fight. Take your positions; then stand still and watch the Lord's victory. He is with you, O people of Judah and Jerusalem. Do not be afraid or discouraged. Go out against them tomorrow, for the Lord is with you!" (2 Chronicles 20:17). Oh, people will make fun of you? God will take care of them. Oh, your parents don't believe in you? God will take care of them. Oh, you have anxiety? God will take care of it. The fear of our battles is just a stumbling block... Jump over it!

When our faith begins to overshadow our fear, we will be unstoppable. We will be like King Hezekiah in the Bible, the king of Judah. 2 Kings 18:6-7 tells us that, "He remained faithful to the Lord in everything, and he carefully obeyed all the commands the Lord had given Moses. So, the Lord was with him, and Hezekiah was successful in everything he did..." Yes, there are so many things to fear in this world, especially the fear of things not working out the way you want them to. But, in the Bible, Paul tells us, "And we know that in all things God works for the good of those who love him, who have been called according to his purpose" (Romans 8:28). I pray that today you break free from the bondage of fear and live your best life in Christ.

You a Black Girl, Too?

Disclaimer: This chapter is not intended to leave anyone out. I'm simply just addressing tests and trials that all Jesus-loving, African-American girls face. Everyone wants someone to relate to.

I live in a small town that is not extremely culturally diverse. Much of my high school is Caucasian. Now, I love every race there is out there, because I know that at heart we are all one, we are all children of God, and we all bleed the same. This world has created so many stereotypes that makes it hard to simply be who you are. Something I've struggled with is people saying I'm "white at heart" or I "act white." They were, of course, saying this because, with Christ in me, I didn't act like the other black people in my school. This, however, did not give them an excuse to classify black people as "hoodrats" that never know how to be nice or presentable. The people would deny it if confronted, but they were basically implying that Caucasian people are the only ones that can have home training or live like Jesus. You might say, "Oh, I'm sure they didn't mean it like that," but I'm telling you that whether they believe it or accept it, that's what they meant. If there is any other interpretation, feel free to let me know. I, of course, forgive everyone that has stereotyped my culture, but if there is just one other black girl that was (or is) ridiculed for her faith in Christ, I want you to know that you're not alone. The stereotypes might make you feel like your race and lifestyle don't line up, but God says it does.

Don't think I forgot about the young, black men out there. It's worse for you guys. There are people out there that will never know the feeling of being judged before you even get the chance to express yourself. Right now, racism is still very much alive, and it can even happen in church! As African-Americans in this day in age, it hurts when people don't understand that we may not have had to pick cotton like our ancestors, but it's still a part of who we are, we are still the minority in most occasions, and we still sometimes feel separated or belittled by everyone else. You might say, "But it's 2018? (Or whatever year you read this book)." If things have changed, there wouldn't be a need for a "Black Lives Matter" movement. Things have progressed, but not completely changed. I pray that none of my fellow young, black disciples ever get discouraged in their walk with Christ because of someone treating them like someone they're not or someone they're "supposed" to be in the eyes of the world. God made all of us and He doesn't make mistakes. I love you ALL, and if you're another race reading this, I truly hope it changed your perspective if it wasn't already where it was supposed to be. God bless y'all... #melanindrippin

Saved

I asked an old friend of mine what he thought being a Christian meant, and he said, "just being a good person." He's that average person whose family doesn't go to church, but they aren't necessarily "bad people." This opened my eyes to see what I believe most people perceive of Christians and they never learn the true gospel, therefore, they miss out on what it truly means to have life in Christ. My old friend didn't know that being saved meant that he would dedicate his life to Christ. I remember being a young girl at an Easter egg hunt on a Saturday morning in Johnson City, Tennessee. All of us little kids were waiting patiently to go outside to hunt eggs, when one of the children's church pastors walked to the front and started talking. The only things I remember him saying is, "Repeat after me," and after repeating all the words he needed to say he said to all of us, "Now when you go home, you can tell your parents and all your family that you've been saved." I remember feeling a little excited even though I didn't really know the dynamics of it. I just knew that being saved was something Christians did in their lifetime, so I was basically just checking it off my list of life. As I grew up and started understanding it more, I always kinda had this fear that me getting saved at the Easter egg hunt didn't count, therefore, every time I was at church and the pastor lead people into getting saved, I would repeat after him. I was a shy kid, and I always hated that preachers would want you to go up to the altar afterwards to get prayed for. Each time that I prayed the prayer and didn't go up to the altar, I felt like it didn't count. I didn't know for a long time that God had already started a work within me while I was a little girl sitting in a chair waiting to hunt Easter eggs. I now realize that even at a young age the devil will attack and tell lies because he feared what would happen if I knew that God called me His child.

Now, if you've been reading this and you haven't accepted Jesus Christ into your life, or maybe you're not sure if you have, I just want to give you the opportunity. This is between you and God, so don't feel like you have to have a whole congregation watching you to make it valid. Say this prayer:

Dear Heavenly Father,

I believe that you sent your son, Jesus Christ, to die for my sins on the cross, and raised him from the dead on the third day. I confess all my sins and invite you into my life. Come into my heart, Lord. Create a new person within me. I love you. In Jesus' name I pray. Amen.

The Bible says that if you prayed that prayer and truly believed it in your heart, you are now a part of the body of Christ. If you didn't dedicate your life today and have never, tomorrow isn't promised, but if there is a tomorrow, Jesus will still be chasing after you.

Christians that walk by the religion of Christianity and not the lifestyle, scare people into believing that they must be perfect to inherit the kingdom of God. It's believed all over the world in churches that if you sin, you're going to hell. It's sad because people will serve God and try their hardest not to sin out of fear of hell, not out of love for God. What these churches fail to tell them is that Jesus already died for ALL our sins. Let me rephrase that: these churches will preach Jesus dying on the cross and even praise Him for it, but they don't preach the full benefit of it. I don't know if you've ever been told this, but you do not go to hell for sinning. I know it's crazy to think about because that's all the religious people try to tell you, but people go to hell for not believing that our gracious God sent His only son, Jesus, to die on the cross <u>for our sins</u>. In the Bible, Romans 6:23 says, "For the wages of sin is death, but the gift of God is eternal life in Christ Jesus our Lord." Before Jesus, God saw that us humans could just not stop sinning, so, instead of all of us dying for our sins, He sent one official sacrifice. Through Jesus Christ, we have eternal life.

It took me a long time to receive in my heart that I didn't have to be perfect to be a child of God. I used to feel like if I made mistakes or sinned, my worthiness in the kingdom of God lowered. I felt like He was mad at me and got tired of me always asking for forgiveness. If that's you right now, God wants you to know that He loves you and He'll never get tired of you running back to Him. To be honest, I was scared to come out with this book because I felt like since God was using me, I couldn't make as many mistakes. He then led me to the story of Noah in the Bible. When we're young, they teach us about Noah and the ark, and since Noah found favor in the Lord's eyes, God didn't destroy him and his family in the flood along with the rest of the people in the land. God used Noah to restart the human race, and what they don't tell us is that Noah got drunk. In the Bible, Genesis 9:21 tells us, "When he drank some of its wine, he became drunk and lay uncovered inside his tent." God showed me that in the very beginning He would use people to further His kingdom and even they would mess up. They didn't even have as many temptations as we do now. God uses imperfection. Dedicating our lives to Christ doesn't mean that we are always sin-free, it means that we recognize that even though we sin sometimes, God looks past all of it and calls us His own. In the middle of all your mess ups, insecurities, and brokenness, Christ is there. Jesus, the perfect one, says, "I have come to call not those who think they are righteous, but those who know they are sinners and need to repent" (Luke 5:32). A relationship with God comes with you being real with him. So many people in the Bible were redeemed simply because they came to Christ as who they truly were. For example: In the Bible, Mark 2:15-16 tells us that Jesus was eating dinner with "tax collectors and other disreputable sinners." The religious people didn't like it and Mark 2:17 says, "When Jesus heard this, he told them, 'Healthy people don't need a doctor - sick people do. I have come to call not those who think they are righteous, but those who know they are sinners.'" I am saved, but I sin. I don't always walk through my high school's halls sharing the love of Christ. Am I going to hell? No, because I know that Jesus already went to hell and back because He knew of all the times I would fall short of the glory of God. That, of course, does not mean that what we do does not matter. I try my hardest not to sin because of my love for God and He is working on me daily. I don't know if this is speaking

83

to anyone because a lot of you are probably already saved and know all of this… but, if there's even just one person that needs to hear this, I'm gonna be obedient to God. Come to Him with who you are. He wants to pour out to you all His blessings and grace. You are NOT too far gone. Jesus says, "In the same way, there is more joy in heaven over one lost sinner who repents and returns to God that over ninety-nine others who are righteous and haven't strayed away!" (Luke 15:7). Let Him change your life. I don't know your story, but I know God wants you to let Him write the rest of it. You may feel like who you are, or your circumstances keep you away from God, but Colossians 3:11 tells us, "In this new life, it doesn't matter if you are a Jew or Gentile, circumcised or uncircumcised, barbaric, uncivilized, slave, or free. Christ is all that matters, and he lives in all of us."

If I've just been telling you what you already know this whole time, I just want to encourage you on your journey. This world is broken, and God has called us to make it whole again. If you still haven't made the decision to have Christ as your Lord and Savior, I wanna give you another opportunity:

Dear Heavenly Father,

I believe that you sent your son, Jesus Christ, to die for my sins on the cross, and raised him from the dead on the third day. I confess all my sins and invite you into my life. Come into my heart, Lord. Create a new person within me. I love you. In Jesus' name I pray, Amen.

In the Bible, Romans 10:13 tells us, "For whoever calls on the name of the Lord shall be saved." People will see something different in you as you walk the halls of your high school. There are going to be battles, but just know that heaven and the body of Christ is rooting for you. I'm praying for all of us young people out here. Let's be the generation that is in this world, but not of it.

Closing

Well, as a pastor I love always says, I'm about to land this plane. If you've made it through this whole book, I just want to thank you for hearing what a God-fearing, imperfect, teenage girl had to say. I would like to thank everyone who has supported me by buying this book and everyone that helped write it whether they knew it or not. Sometimes, you just need a little help on your spiritual journey and I would like to thank: Rooted Youth Church, Judah Church, Trigg Street Church, my dad, Heather Lindsey (her YouTube videos), Transformation Church (YouTube videos), and Jesus for being my help. I'm sure everything in this book couldn't apply to everyone because we are all different. I'm no prophet. I'm simply just a young girl trying to glorify God and lead people to His kingdom. I pray that God was able to speak to you in some way through this book and if you took a big step by dedicating your life to Christ through the "Saved" chapter, feel free to message me on any social media platform. I'd really love to know and answer any questions you might have. I love and encourage everyone on their walk with Christ and pray that us young disciples can take over the world... all we need to do is love. I don't know if you had a good day, but the Bible says, "This is the day the Lord has made. We will rejoice and be glad in it" (Psalms 118:24).

Also, small shout out to the Virginia High School class of 2019! It's our last year in prison and I just wanna encourage you guys for wherever God leads you next. I may not have appreciated all of you guys being in my class, but I love ya! And God loves ya! Amen!

Made in the USA
Middletown, DE
21 November 2018